About the Author

Andrew is a solicitor in private practice, specialising in real estate and construction disputes. He has published various legal books and articles and holds an associate professorship at a university where he tutors land law part-time. Married with two adult sons, Andrew's passions are Saracens, golf and playing the piano (very badly). Andrew would like to collaborate with one or more composers who are willing to put poems within this collection to music with the aim of producing a theatrical work. If you are interested in collaborating with Andrew, please contact him.

Horatio Nelson: A Hero's Life in Rhyme

Andrew Olins

Horatio Nelson: A Hero's Life in Rhyme

Vanguard Press

VANGUARD PAPERBACK

© Copyright 2025
Andrew Olins

The right of Andrew Olins to be identified as author of
this work has been asserted by him in accordance with the
Copyright, Designs and Patents Act 1988.

All Rights Reserved

No reproduction, copy or transmission of this publication
may be made without written permission.
No paragraph of this publication may be reproduced,
copied or transmitted save with the written permission of the publisher, or in
accordance with the provisions
of the Copyright Act 1956 (as amended).

Any person who commits any unauthorised act in relation to this publication
may be liable to criminal prosecution and civil claims for damages.

A CIP catalogue record for this title is available from the British Library.

ISBN 978-1-83794-373-9

This is a work of fiction. Names, characters, businesses, places, events and
incidents are either the products of the author's imagination or used in a
fictitious manner. Any resemblance to actual persons, living or dead, or actual
events is purely coincidental.

Vanguard Press is an imprint of
Pegasus Elliot Mackenzie Publishers Ltd.
www.pegasuspublishers.com

First Published in 2025

Vanguard Press
Sheraton House Castle Park
Cambridge England

Printed & Bound in Great Britain

Dedication

I dedicate this work to all would-be heroes. "Don't be found despairing in moments of doubt, nor wanting courage to turnabout."

Acknowledgements

Andrew would like to thank his parents, Leone and Michael, for their support and encouragement in producing this collection of poems. Nonic and Chop Chop, and for my next project...

Market Day

Nelson, as a young boy, strolls through a nearby Norfolk village, Burnham Overy Staithe. May 1770

Is this our hero, an inquisitive boy
Taking a stroll through Burnham Thorpe?
It's market day, the liveliest of affairs
With local craftsmen peddling their wares.

Beaux and belles skip round Maypoles
As older folk stop to cheer.
Travelling acrobats display their fitness
'Tis a joyous scene for the village to witness!

Is that our hero, heading for the quay?
To spy on a lugger returned to port?
Crates are hoisted, "heave" is the cry,
Sweat is dripping, and mouths are dry.

"You may now go ashore," the chief mate barks.
"Here's your pay, twenty shillings each."
"Wear proper clothing, take your fleece."
Riotous lot, won't keep the peace.

Is that our hero, shadowing the crew

To satisfy his curiosity?
He's being led to rougher parts
Where the streets are too narrow for horse-drawn carts.

Fancy ladies appear at first-floor windows
As the crew passes by below.
Beware, Horatio; be astute,
Eschew girls of ill repute.

Is that our hero entering a tavern?
To share a pint with sailors downing eight?
To feast on their stories of far-off lands
And ships that floundered on the sands?

Observe Horatio, his eyes tell it all.
Spellbound, captivated, enthralled.
A fuse has been lit.
To life at sea, he'll now commit.

Au Revoir

Nelson quits home to join the Navy. 1770

Dearest Papa,

I shan't be following you into the Church
As I'll never possess the gifts for your vocation.
If, in your eyes, I have fallen off my perch
Understand that I must find my own salvation.

My heart lies with the sea.
I want its rising and falling waves to decide my fate.
I go to enlist in the Royal Navy.
Please, Papa, don't be too irate.

Before I sleep at night
I shall look skywards towards the North Star,
Knowing however perilous my plight
This not goodbye, but au revoir.

Your devoted son,
Horatio.

Join Raisonnable

Nelson joins *HMS Raisonnable,* captained by his uncle, Maurice Suckling. A ship's officer seeks to recruit ratings. 1770

If you are brave and fearless, come here and listen.
Not you, sir, old and wizen.
Nor you, newly freed from prison.
I address men strong in mind and body
Who crave adventure and Spaniards to disembody.
Come join Captain Suckling on aboard the good ship, *Raisonnable*
And serve as a landsman as best as you're able.

A sailor's life is not for the fainthearted.
We sail to distant waters never charted.
And consign Frenchies to the dearly departed!
Take a break from ploughing cornfields and the Sunday pew
Enjoy the camaraderie of our merry crew.
Come join Captain Suckling on aboard the good ship, *Raisonnable*
And serve as a landsman as best as you're able.

A sailor courageously goes where angels fear to tread.

Oy, keep a civil tongue in your head.
Our country's fortunes hang by a thread.
If you want rum on tap, a weekly quart,
And a willing lover in every port,
Come join Captain Suckling on aboard the good ship,
Raisonnable
And serve as a landsman as best as you're able.

On-Board Raisonnable

The treatment of press-ganged ratings. 1770

Being a rating means tolerating
Cramped dorms and hurricane storms
And enemy mortars fired from close quarters.
Being a rating means tolerating
Worm-ridden grub and no bathtub
And blisters from a whip swung from the hip.
Being a rating means tolerating
Sleepless nights and climbing masts to dangerous heights
And disease that makes the blood freeze.

Raisonnable Is Paid-off

HMS *Raisonnable*, Nelson's first ship, is paid off. Captain Suckling addresses the ship's company. 1773

Attention.
I have received a signal from the Admiralty, which I must mention.
After five months patrolling these waters, *Raisonnable* is to be paid-off.
No more stand-off.
For now, the risk of war with Spain is over.
We're heading back to Dover.
You've served faithfully and, I dare say, a few will be missed.
Extra rum today, but don't get too pissed.
Dismissed.

Suckling's Advice

Nelson is offered advice by his uncle, Maurice Suckling, on how to become an officer. 1773

Nephew. A word of advice, if I may?

To make officer grade, you could try the Triangular Trade.
But trafficking slaves is demeaning and vile
Conducted by merchants who say with guile
It's a necessary evil: thinking that's truly primeval.
So, you could cast around for a ship Africa-bound.

Rumours abound of an Arctic expedition, a scientific mission
Led by Constance Phipps of the vessel, *Racehorse*
To discover a Northeast Passage and chart a course
To India and the Pacific; joining such a voyage would be terrific.
Think of the knowledge you would gain, even as a lowly coxswain.

Uncle Maurice knows best.
Heed my advice to attain your quest.

Arctic Expedition

Nelson and the Bear

Nelson joins *Carcass* on a scientific expedition to the North Pole. Summer 1773

Two bomb ships, veterans of hostility
Under the patronage of nobility
Strengthened and refitted,
And with scientific equipment kitted,
Raise anchor at Little Nore
Tasked to discover a northeast corridor.

Foregoing the protection of the Thames estuary
Carcass and *Racecourse* head for open sea.
Bidding farewell to England's summer weather
Of brittle bracken and scorched heather,
Into the Atlantic Ocean, they set forth
Setting a course of magnetic north.

The Arctic Circle sneers at summertime
And *Carcass*' captain misjudges the clime.
When nearing Svalbard's western coast
Captain Lutwidge is not at his post.
Unaware of approaching ice
The ship is imprisoned in a glacial vice.

There is nothing that the crew can do, but sit and wait
And ponder their fate.
Under their breath, they curse Lutwidge for his crime,
And play *Maw* and *Piquet* to pass the time.
To relieve his boredom, our hero volunteers for patrol.
Musket in hand, he's eager to stroll.

Spotting a polar bear, Horatio declares, "What a beauty."
"Its skin will make handsome booty."
Striding forwards, our hero stumbles,
His musket misfires, and the beast rumbles.
A volley of shots from on-board makes the bear draw back.
Horatio is thus saved from fatal attack.

With wounded pride, our hero returns to *Carcass*,
Expecting to be rebuked for being an ass.
But Lutwidge's bark is worse than his bite
He shows leniency to the contrite.
Horatio apologises and is dismissed
With no more than a slap on the wrist.

Showing pity, the Arctic relents
Welcome relief for *Carcass*' malcontents.
As the glacial vice eases its grip
Thoughts dissolve of abandoning ship.
Elusive is the Holy Grail
In discovering a northeast corridor, the ships fail.

Why does this voyage excite the imagination?
Is it illustrative of the spirit of a nation?
Or is it the escapade of a lowly coxswain
Who, through impulsiveness, was almost slain?
Whatever the reason, to John Landseer we must say, "Thank you."
For immortalising pictorially, our hero's derring-do.

Promotion

Nelson takes the Admiralty's examination to become an officer: 1777

Nelson
Leading by example means being willing to put oneself in harm's way.

Examiner 2
A further question Midshipman Nelson, if I may? I have read the reports in this dossier. Your courageous deeds never fail to impress. Of course, one man's courage is another's foolhardiness. On this question, what do you say?

Nelson
The difference between the two, sir, is one of success or failure. No more, no less.

Suckling
If there are no further questions, you may retire whilst we deliberate.

Examiner 2

Well, sirs, let's settle this man's fate. I have an evening engagement and it's getting late.

Examiner 3
Without doubt, this midshipman displays leadership potential. Amongst his peers, he is, I understand, quite influential.

Examiner 2
To his superiors, he could be more deferential!

Examiner 3
There is no enemy of the king, he would shun.

Suckling
I have a confession to make about Midshipman Nelson. He's my nephew, my sister's son.

Examiner 2
Pray tell, why you have till now concealed this fact? Were you troubled about how we might react?

Suckling
I had no desire to influence your decision. I was confident he'd pass the examination with distinction. Admittedly, he's my kinsman, but in Horatio, I sense a man with vision.

Examiner 3
Well, the boy has my support.

Examiner 2
If I'd been the captain of *Carcass*, I would have hauled him before a disciplinary court. Taking on a polar bear is hardly innocent sport.

Suckling
It's adolescence.

Examiner 3
And barely a capital offence.

Examiner 2
Where is his maturity and common sense?

Suckling
Privateers imperil our Atlantic trade routes. Who do you propose we dispatch to defeat these lawless brutes?

Examiner 3
Young, fearless recruits.

Suckling
Indeed.

Examiner 3
Are we now agreed?

Examiner 2

If this is going to be his first campaign, we had better wish Lieutenant Nelson, God's speed.

Letter Home

Nelson writes to his father on passing the Admiralty's examination to become an officer. 1777

Dearest Papa,

Far from going astray
Your boy made lieutenant today!
I'm not expecting you to raise a cheer
Knowing your disapproval of my chosen career.

I shall have my new uniform tailor-made
Following the fashion of velvet and gold braid.
Looking the part in my case is vital;
Our family possessing no hereditary title.

I sail for the West Indies before the month-end
On board *Lowestoffe*, which has orders to defend
British cargo from pirates so brazen-faced
They kill, plunder and lay waste.

I cannot in all honesty disguise
My excitement of sharing a vast prize.
This incentive can only heighten the rapture
Of engaging pirate ships and securing their capture.

Before I depart
May we draw a line and make a new start?
I long to be received in Kent.
Do I have your consent?

Your devoted son,

Horatio

Raiding Party

A raiding party, which includes Nelson, makes camp along the infested San Juan River, Nicaragua.1779

Such an insidious sound
Rising from the mire;
It's the sound of vibrating wings
Drawn to a raiding party's campfire.

Such an insidious sound
Readying to feed;
It's the sound of parasitic insects
Piercing the skin, sucking the bleed.

Such an insidious sound
Heard in the morn;
It's the sound of brothers in arms
Waking feverish and forlorn.

Such an insidious sound
In the heat of the day;
It's the sound of burying comrades
Before their bodies decay.

Such an insidious sound
Retreating back to ship;
It's the sound of dragging boots
Of territorial gains allowed to slip.

Yellow Jack Fever

Nelson returns home to England after contracting Yellow Jack Fever. 1779

Nelson
Is that you, Cornwallis, my faithful friend?
A radiant orb is beckoning.
I'm earnest, Billy; please no derision.
Am I blessed or cursed by this brilliant vision?
What does it portend?

Come take my hand, warm my hand
Ease my shallow breathing.
I'm frightened, Billy, I'm stony cold.
I fear Yellow Jack has taken hold.
Will I survive to see dryland?

Cornwallis
The radiant orb beckons you home
To your beloved Burnham Thorpe.
Your faithful friend will care for you
And with God's grace, you will pull through.
I'm here, Horatio, you're not alone.

First Love

Nelson meets his first love in Québec. 1781

If my heart and head spoke with one voice
Harmony, not discord, would reign.
And I'd be spared a torment
Which I'm struggling to contain.

The cause of this torment
Is a girl so charming, so full of grace,
To prove my worth,
There's no trial I'd decline to face.

Yet, by proposing to this girl
I risk my parents' scorn.
With little schooling in the arts
They'll assuredly view her lowborn.

And if I offer marriage
To a girl with no dowry,
My fellow officers will surely mock
My choice of bride-to-be.

Yet, I could act chivalrously
Treating the mockers with disdain.

And like knights of old
Play the ardent swain.

I arrived in Quebec feeling subdued
Symptoms of a tropical infection.
And her gentle smile and amorous gaze
Has cured my introspection.

Yet, if I marry in haste
I could repent at leisure.
And hazard this awakening first love
Descending to displeasure.

With a promising naval career
Why should I rush to wed?
I must accept the counsel of caution
And subordinate heart to head.

Role Play

At a dinner party in the West Indies on board *HMS Boreas*, which Nelson commands, the guests ruminate on the roles played by the diplomat, warrior and chaplain in times of crisis. 1784

Who will be disarming
In the face of provocation?
One who is effective
In diffusing escalation.
No amount of abuse
Would cause him to let loose
The lightning bolts of Zeus.
He is the diplomat.

Who will be opposing
In the face of onslaught?
One who risks ultimate sacrifice
Without a passing thought.
His kinsmen will he shield,
Never to quit the field
Whatever the weapon wield.
He is the warrior.

Who will be uplifting

In the face of hostility?
One who can reassure
That war has utility.
The enemy he will impeach.
The justice of the cause will he preach.
To God, victory he will beseech.
He is the chaplain.

Proposal

Frances Nelson, First Viscountess Nelson

Nelson proposes marriage to the widow, Frances Nisbet, on the Island of Nevis in the Caribbean. 1786

Nelson
Throw off your widow's weeds,
Put them on this well-lit fire.
Marry me, dearest Fanny
Surrender to your heart's desire.

There is no virtue being alone,
Abandon respectful piety.
Marry me, dearest Fanny
Re-engage in good society.

Quit this house of sad remembrance,
Settle in Norfolk, God's own land.
Marry me, dearest Fanny
Witness Burham's sea-strand.

Give Josiah an honest father,
Before he's fully grown.
Marry me, dearest Fanny,
I'll treat him as my own.

Prince William will be best man,
If the ceremony is next spring.
Marry me, dearest Fanny
Accept this engagement ring.

Life should be an epic adventure,
Embrace this man of deeds.
Marry me, dearest Fanny
Come, burn your widow's weeds.

Fanny
What will your family say?

Nelson
My family will adore you.
Wealthy father on the bench!
Marry me, dearest Fanny
Be my beautiful, intelligent, wench.

Wedding Vows

Fanny's wedding vow to Nelson. Montpelier Estate, Nevis. 11 March 1787

Blessed, blessed vow
To be the perfect sailor's wife
To be the anchor in his life.
When he's restless on dry land
And yearning for a new command.

Blessed, blessed vow
To be the perfect sailor's wife
To be the compass in his life.
When vanity threatens his life story
In reckless pursuit of naval glory.

Blessed, blessed vow
To be the perfect sailor's wife
To be the rudder in his life.
When the allure of capturing a valuable prize
Makes the brutality of war harder to despise.

Blessed, blessed vow
To be the perfect sailor's wife
To be the mast in his life.

When he's tossed about by life's travails
And self-doubt draws wind from his sails.

Blessed, blessed vow
To be the perfect sailor's wife
To be the figurehead in his life.
When the cannons fall silent after a battle hard-fought
Leading him safely home to port.

Emma's Ballroom Entrance

Emma, Lady Hamilton

Nelson meets Emma, Lady Hamilton, whilst on a diplomatic mission to Naples. 1792

Aren't I the beauty, the belle of the ball?
My admirers are many as I enter the hall.
As they plead for my dance card, I fear a brawl.
How I love the attention; I aim to enthral.

Aren't I the lucky girl? I bagged a baronet.
Not bad for a blacksmith's daughter, born to know debt.
As consort to Sir William, I exude poise and etiquette.
How I delight befriending the premier set.

Aren't I the fancy lady? My rivals muse,
"To get ahead, there's no man she'd refuse."
I'm not proud of my past, but I must disabuse,
The men that I bed, I carefully choose.

Aren't I the dancer, a true pearl?
I glide effortlessly as I pivot and twirl,
Giddily falling into the arms of an earl.
How, I wonder, will this evening unfurl?

I Got a Little Hurt This Morning

Nelson writes to his wife, Fanny, after being injured defending Corsica from the French in December 1793.

My dearest Fanny
I got a little hurt this morning
As you may judge from this epistle.
While inspecting batteries at Calvi
My right eye was hurt by an exploding missile.
I can see very well with the left
So, there's no fear of honourable dismissal.
Yet, I'm confined to sickbay until I heal.
Perhaps I'll practise a tune on the boatswain's whistle?

The war goes badly in the Mediterranean.
How maddening it is to be on the run!
Should Corsica fall
Our blockade by sea will be undone.
And without a blockade, I venture to ask:
How's this wretched war to be won?
We're keeping faith in Hood to reverse our fortunes.
He's a man not easily outdone.

I witnessed horror at Toulon hard to describe.
Axes in hand, a mob rose

Cutting down innocents in their hundreds.
What motivates the Gallic race? Satan knows!
How different are the English.
Through our veins, mercy flows.
We do not kill for killing's sake.
Only in the face of evil do we oppose.

You'll be anxious for word of Josiah.
Well, I'm glad to be his mentor.
As midshipman on-board *Agamemnon*
Your son, the boy, is no more.
He's diligent, dependable,
And gamely steps to the fore.
Proudly, I introduce him as my own.
Be assured, Josiah is having an excellent war.

Yours ever

Horatio

King and Country

Nelson opines on 'King and Country' following his injury defending Corsica. December 1793

Love of king and country
Won't create paradise.
But, in advancing the commonwealth,
Its defence warrants sacrifice.

First Prize

Nelson, as captain of *HMS Agamemnon*, speaks to one of his lieutenants after capturing his first prize in The Battle of Genoa, fought between the British and French fleets in March 1795.

Four hundred casualties! You say.
And half of them dead.
Good heavens!
Her deck must be stained blood red.

Why didn't she strike her colours?
She'd no place to hide.
She was well beaten
By *Agamemnon's* rapid broadside.

I pity *Ça Ira's* captain.
He's a big disgrace.
Sacrificing lives
Vainly trying to save face.

She's a perfect wreck, you say.
Masks and rigging down.
How dispiriting!
The prize will be half a crown.

More Frenchmen were for the taking.
Why call off the pursuit?
No vision!
Lord Hothan deserves the boot.

If I'd been the admiral
The fleet I'd have loosed.
And had such a day
As England ever produced.

Battle of Cape St Vincent

Rear-Admiral, Sir John Jervis, Earl of St Vincent

Fought between the British and Spanish fleets off the
Portuguese peninsular. 14 February 1797

Prelude to the Battle, January 1797

Up and down the kingdom there's much trepidation
Spawned by the quickening beat of foreign drumming.
All Britain cries with a single voice
"Help us, Lord; the Spanish and French are coming."

Undercover spies learn of the allies' plan
For Britain's cruel and unsparing subjugation.
Their two fleets will rendezvous near Brest
From where they'll launch an invasion.

On receiving this unnerving intelligence
Prime Minister Pitt fears conquest and tyranny.
His demands of the Navy are blunt:
"Stop the Spanish; they mustn't reach Brittany."

Instructions are dispatched to the fleet off Tagus,
Commanded by the devout Admiral Jervis.
Dutifully, he raises anchor
After priestly blessings at Morning Service.

February

While approaching the narrow Strait of Gibraltar
Spain's Admirante Córdoba curses his ill luck.
Blown off course by a fierce laventer

For several days, his Armada comes unstuck.

The scattered Spanish hastily reassemble
Directly the windstorm loses its aggression.
And twenty-seven ships of the line
Haughtily resume their stately procession.

Intending to replenish declining supplies
Córdoba heads for Spanish-controlled Cadiz Bay,
But an impenetrable fog forms
Putting another obstacle in his way.

11 February

The pea-souper offers excellent camouflage
For Jervis' hunting, searching fleet.
Noble on *Minerve* spots the Spanish
And unobserved hurriedly makes a retreat.

Knowing the importance of his discovery
Noble hies to Jervis' flagship, *Victory*.
Clasping the captain's hand, Jervis vows
"Let's make Córdoba's Armada history."

Jervis' fifteen assorted ships of the line
Bravely sally forth, impatient to intercept.
Facing far greater firepower
They must prove themselves more adept.

*Nelson boarding 'San Nicolas' at the Battle of Cape St Vincent,
14 February 1797*

14 February 7 A.M.
Against the backdrop of daybreak's faint horizon
Five languid silhouettes are observed wallowing.

Troubridge on *Culloden* leads the chase
With the rest of the fleet keenly following.

Becoming discernible five miles off
Córdoba's Armada certainly impresses.
Split in two loose, uneven columns
Of eighteen and nine, Jervis guesses.

11:30 A.M.

The column of nine lies leeward to the eighteen
And closer to Troubridge and the chasing pack.
Córdoba is evidently ill-prepared
Making him vulnerable to sudden attack.

Jervis orders his fleet to sail through the Spanish
Forcing Córdoba's unwitting columns to bunch.
Firing canons in both directions
The English make the most of their lesser punch.

Anxious to press home his tactical advantage
Jervis promptly orders his ships to come about.
By re-engaging the leeward nine
He sees a possibility to win out.

Once more, *Culloden* fronts a renewed attack

With *Blenheim* and *Prince George* a short distance behind.
But one officer flouts his orders
Exhibiting unrivalled presence of mind.

Positioned towards the rear of the fleet
Nelson on *Captain* abandons his place in the line.
He foresees an indecisive draw
If, windward, the two Spanish columns combine.

1 P.M.

Resolving to bedevil the windward eighteen
Nelson tells his helmsman to bring *Captain* around.
Passing by *Diadem* and *Excellent*
He sails his seventy-four-gunner westbound.

With the eighteen's midpoint cluster, his prime target
Nelson navigates to cut right cross their bows.
Ignorant of his calculation
On *Victory*, there are several raised eyebrows.

1:30 P.M.

Jervis signals his hindmost vessel, *Excellent*
To come to wind directly on the larboard tack.
In getting ahead of *Culloden*
Her commander, Collingwood, doesn't hold back.

As the leeward nine are gradually overhauled
Troubridge begins discharging *Culloden's* lockers.

And *Blenheim* and *Prince George* sail windward
To lie between the two columns as blockers.

1:45 P.M.

Captain brings her well-drilled firing to bear
As she cheerily torments the midpoint cluster.
With telling hits to their upper decks
Four wounded Spaniards are left in a fluster.

Yet, Nelson feels his ship's sacrifice acutely
From *Santisima Trinidad's* countering blasts.
With her one hundred and thirty guns
Córdoba's flagship wrecks *Captain's* sails and masts.

Excellent hurriedly comes to *Captain's* rescue
Drawing *Santisima Trinidad's* broadside shots.
Able to make essential repairs
Captain's crew slices with reef and bowline knots.

2:30 P.M.

After patching her running rigging
Captain is soon able to return to the fray.
As the crew reload the ship's canons
Jervis orders *Excellent* to edge away.

Arriving abreast of *Salvador del Mundo*
Collingwood aims his fire towards the weather bow.
After trading shots for some minutes

The gravely holed Spaniard keeps afloat somehow.

Still flustered after *Captain* blew off her top masts,
Collingwood eyes *San Ysido* for her prize.
Despite a truly gallant defence
This Spaniard surrenders to avoid capsize.

Excellent next combines with incoming *Diadem*
To re-engage hapless *Salvator del Mundo*.
Hit from weather bow and lee quarter
This teetering Spaniard strikes her colours too.

3 P.M.
Falling upon *San Nicolás*, *Captain* lets loose
Inflicting damage to the Spaniard's foretop mast.
With a third ship at risk of capture
Córdoba becomes decidedly downcast.

Joining *Captain's* close assault on *San Nicolás*
Excellent's shots put the Spaniard in disarray.
She luffs up, endeavouring to flee
But, sadly for her, runs foul of *San José*.
Nelson audaciously bids to board both Spaniards
Ramming *San Nicolás'* starboard quarter hard.
Locked together by *Captain's* cat-head
Nelson's battle-toughened boarders won't be barred.

3.20 P.M.

"Westminster Abbey or Glorious Victory!"

Is Nelson's cry as swords are drawn and muskets fired.
As they jump onto *San Nicolás*
These selfless boarders are richly inspired.

Chaotic hand-to-hand combat ensures
On *San Nicolás* and later *San José*.
Facing greater single-mindedness
Initial Spanish resistance falls away.

Coming forward to present their swords to Nelson
Both commandantes bow, signifying submission.
By capturing these two Spanish ships
Nelson proves himself a master tactician.

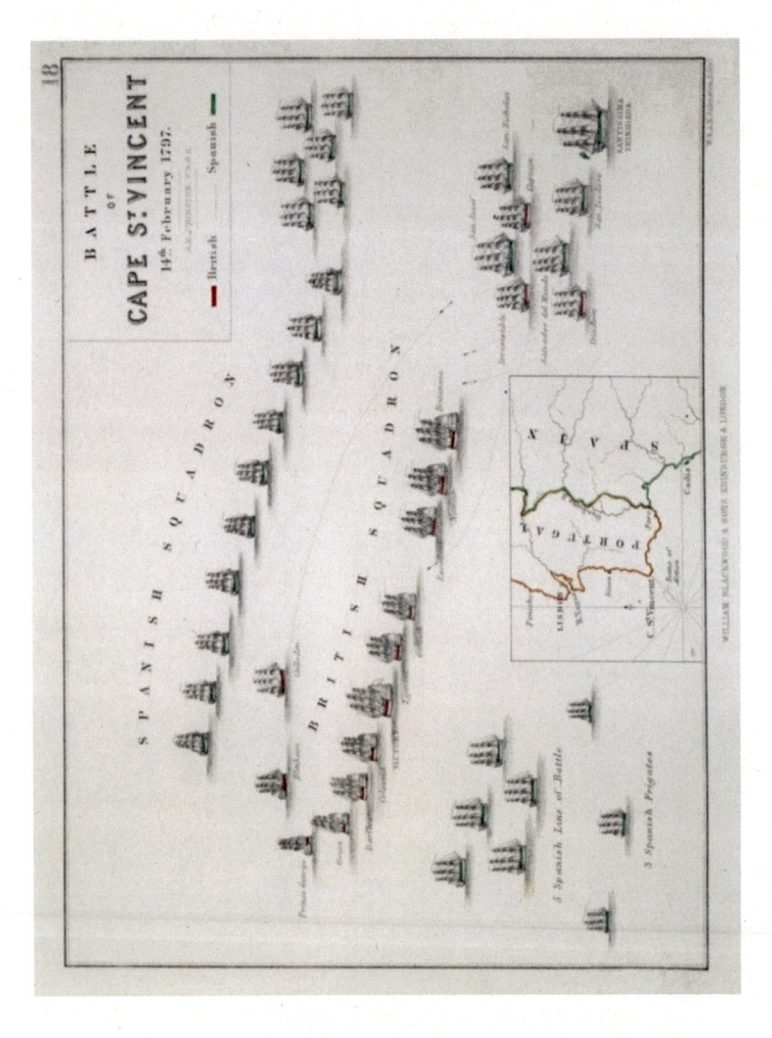

Battle of Cape St Vincent.

4 P.M.

Santisima Trinidad and her escorts flee
Effectively bringing an end to the show.
Córdoba leaves Jervis' frigates
To take the four captured prizes in tow.

End of the battle

Blackened by bellowing smoke in the fighting
Nelson quits *San José's* poop deck, bubbling with joy.
Welcoming him on-board *Victory*
Jervis hails the Navy's new wonder boy.

The Armada suffers six times as many deaths:
Four hundred and thirty versus seventy-three.
Ritual burials at sea begin
As Córdoba's flagship limps to sanctuary.

Aftermath

Jervis' stunning success off Cape St Vincent
Puts the threat of invasion and conquest to bed.
And by blockading Cadiz Bay
The Navy wrests control of the Med.

On the recommendation of a grateful Pitt,
Jervis is raised to the peerage as a reward.
Nelson, too, is publicly honoured
With a knighthood and ceremonial sword.

One hundred and forty thousand pounds was the total prize
Shared amongst all officers and ratings who fought.
No more is heard of Admirante Córdoba
Having been promptly dismissed from court.

*Nelson Fighting a Spanish Launch at Cadiz
14 February 1797*

The Reverend's Letter

Reverend Edmund Nelson writes to his son, Horatio, following the Battle of Cape St Vincent. May 1797

My Dear Horatio

I supped with my Lord Bishop last night.
He, being recently returned from Westminster, brought news of your deeds.
He had a newspaper; I could barely believe how it reads.
So fulsome is the praise, I felt constrained to write.

Under a banner 'Nelson's Patent Bridge for boarding first-rates'
It describes, most graphically, how you wrested two enemy ships.
Did you board with "Westminster Abbey or Glorious Victory" on your lips?
Whether or not that is so, you are put amongst the Navy's living greats.

I confessed to my Lord Bishop: Is this my son?
The Horatio I spawned surely could not be so brave.
Perhaps you were seized by the prospect of valuable prizes, which, I know, you crave?

Be that as it may, I shun the thought of you in close combat with sword or gun.

The article concludes with a demand that your heroics be recognised.
Echoing, I am told, similar calls in the House of Peers a week ago.
But what honour to bestow?
As my Lord Bishop remarked, we can be confident that you won't be canonised!

In persisting with our estrangement, I confess to behaving stubbornly.
I should take pride in your career.
By all accounts, you will rise to a height of glory within the year
That few sons attain, and fewer fathers live to see.

I long to receive you.

Your admiring Papa

Santa Cruz

Nelson when wounded at the Battle of Santa Cruz
22- 25 July 1797

Nelson leads a failed attack on Santa Cruz, Tenerife. 21 July 1779

Admiral Sir Horatio Nelson would assuredly agree
He's never had a sorrier day at sea.
He's to be found on board his flagship
Biting hard on his lower lip.
Typical of a warrior not prone to lament,
He endeavours to make light of his predicament.
But don't be mistaken
By a façade, seemingly, unshaken.
Stepson, Josiah, isn't, as he paces the room
Nor the surgeon handing Nelson rum to consume.
Could there be a surgeon with scrubs more bloodstained?
Curious for one reputedly so well-trained.
Admittedly, he's performed ten amputations in two hours
And sawing limbs isn't like cutting wildflowers.
Predictably business-like and lacking finesse
Comes the instruction to Nelson to undress.

'Twas a well-conceived attack to be sprung at night
And with months of planning, supposedly, watertight.
To weaken Spain's grip on her island stronghold,
By seizing ships moored there laden with gold.
But a gale suddenly got up
And, brazenly, wouldn't let up.
Unable to land in darkness undeniably cost
As by morning, the element of surprise was lost.
When a party eventually got ashore which Nelson led
They couldn't secure a crucial beachhead.

And with no covering fire from the sea
Spanish resistance was made all too easy.
Pinned down with a rising attrition rate
The landing party faced an ignominious fate.
There was no alternative but to withdraw
To the nauseating sound of Spanish guffaw.

Doggedness in getting ashore
And selflessness in leading the marine corps.
But fatalities were more than a few
Begging the question, was there foolhardiness too?
Perhaps thoughts of a fantastic prize
Spawned actions which were, in truth, unwise?
Failure came at an awful price
With Nelson, too, sharing the sacrifice.
Whist retreating, he felt a thud
Followed by the sensation of gushing blood.
Hit by grapeshot above the right elbow
Make-do bandages could barely stem the flow.
Quite insensible whilst conveyed back to ship
"I'm a dead man" was Nelson's quip.
Yet the marine corps prayed for their admiral to live
Confident that, in Nelson, they had nothing to forgive.

Such remarkable loyalty can save a man's career
And help him recover from his nadir.

Approaching Dover

Nelson returns to England after four years at sea. 1797

Lookout
Land ahoy, land ahoy.

Lieutenant
Admiral, I sense your joy.

Nelson
I glimpse the White Cliffs and I'm a child reunited with his favourite toy.

Lookout
Land ahoy, land ahoy.

Lieutenant
Enough. We've heard you, boy!

Nelson
Such is my love for England, I'd lay down my life to play a part in her story.

Lieutenant

Dulce et decorum est pro patria mori.

Nelson
A death sweet, proper and crowned in glory. My papa never tires of quoting Horace to lift his oratory. Particularly when threatening his flock with purgatory. I've lost an eye and an arm in the service of my country. Yet, despite these woes, I remain committed to confronting England's foes. Whenever duty calls, I'll sail to oppose.

Lieutenant
To the close. Until you rest in sweet repose.

Nelson
You mock.

Lieutenant
No, Sir. Not at all. I, too, love my country, don't get me wrong. But I wanted comradeship and a desire to belong. I didn't get that growing up in an orphanage, where I scrapped along. That's why I enrolled and my commitment to the Navy is lifelong. When we boarded *San Nicolás*, I was in the throng. And from the start. I'm an adventurer at heart. If I had been shot or run-through that day, like Jones and Cathcart, I would have died knowing I did my part.

Nelson
That would have been an unwelcome fate. Particularly for an aspiring officer who we've come to rate. Take a lead in battle, and by all means, display a buccaneering trait. But remember, an officer has responsibilities he can't abdicate. And recklessly putting one's men in harm's way crosses a line no officer should contemplate.

Lieutenant
I'd never do that. So, no belling the cat?

Nelson
Horace, now Aesop. You, plainly, never wore the dunce's hat.

Lieutenant
Classics was the one subject I excelled at.

Nelson
I loathed it. But then again, we were taught by an autocrat.

Lieutenant
Ours was a retired diplomat. Perhaps a flotilla will come out to welcome us back?

Nelson
After Santa Cruz, my first stop is Admiralty House to take the flack.

Lieutenant
No, sir. What about Cape St Vincent? You deserve a plaque.

Nelson
You'll learn that the Lords Commissioners have short memories. I'll face the pack and, hopefully, avoid the rack. There's something different about the cliffs. Don't you think they appear…

Lieutenant
Austere?

Nelson
Yes.

Lieutenant
They're standing taller, prouder… more severe.

Nelson
The chalk face is a sight every Englishman should revere.

Lieutenant
Yes.

Nelson
Who'll be waiting for you? Anyone?

Lieutenant
No. There're plenty of hearts I could have won. But I like my fun.

Nelson
At your age, I wasn't to be outdone. Too much kiss and run.

Lieutenant
And you, sir. Where will you be heading after…

Nelson
Bath. I'm taking rooms there. With Joseph Spry. I'm putting myself in his care. There's no better apothecary anywhere.

Lieutenant
The perfect cure for the vicissitudes of warfare.

Nelson
The properties of the spa waters are mystical and rare. I'll imbibe and immerse myself and, who knows, I may grow a spare. Moreover, Lady Nelson will enjoy the society. The assembly rooms offer a wide variety. There'll be those who attend court to those who court notoriety. And even the odd bishop exuding piety, extolling the rest of us to behave with propriety.

Lieutenant
Much to amuse.

Nelson
That's for Lady Nelson. I intend to keep myself out of view.

Lieutenant
How will you deter noisy neighbours wanting to hear first-hand tales of your derring-do? Or reporters banging on your door for an interview?

Nelson
Stop it.

Lieutenant
But it's true. You'll need to…

Nelson
What? Lock myself in the master bedroom. Better still, adopt a nom de plume? Or attend the Pump Room in a pantomime costume? I assure you it won't be all gloom. If, in a week or two, you're floundering for something to do, why don't you follow us down? Lady Nelson would be delighted to introduce you across town. Don't frown. You could do a lot worse than chose a wife and settle down. And there're plenty of shops in Bath to buy a bridal gown.

Lieutenant
As long as I can leave my marriage vows at Dover. Mine's the life of a rover.

Nelson
Who wrote, "Atop the Cliffs of Dover, lie fields of sun-warmed clover?"

Lookout
Welcoming boats off the port bow.

Nelson
Apparently, our conversation is over.

Criticism

An unrepentant Nelson responds to criticism following his failed attack on Santa Cruz. 1779

I am Nelson, I am bold
Perhaps too much, if truth be told
In my determination to win.
Yet, I've seen admirals before,
Showing weakness, I deplore.
Never, ever could there be a greater sin.

I inspire, say the crew
Perhaps taken by my derring-do
As I perform nervy tactical plays.
To my critics, I'm reckless
Conceited, even feckless.
How I loathe these feeble-minded popinjays.

Bath, England

Nelson makes light of his injuries. New Year's Day 1798

Most men will despise not having two good arms or eyes
But I'm not one.
I make fun – often winning a prize for my Blackbeard disguise.
As long as I can use this retractable telescope,
Walk a tight rope,
And avoid slipping on scented bath soap,
I'll not mope.
In the best traditions of the Navy, I'll cope!

Injuries to arms and eyes commonly traumatise
But I'm different.
I'm not spent resisting the nation I most despise.
As long as I can brandish my ceremonial sword,
Lead the charge to board,
And, of course, play left-handed the harpsichord,
I'll not groan.
In the best traditions of the Navy, I'll never moan!

Battle of the Nile (Aboukir Bay)

Fought between the British and French fleets off the Nile Delta of Egypt. 1-3 August 1798

Restive after his victorious campaign in Italy
Napoleon returns to Paris to receive his nation's praise.
As he enters the City's Place du Trône
Revolutionaries start singing La Marseillaise.

Days later, the Général unnerves the governing quintet
By boasting at a celebratory feast,
"Europe is far too small a field for me."
"I'll attain great celebrity only in the East."

The quintet daren't confront or mock Napoleon in public
Least he uses his popularity to foment a coup d'etat.
So they resolve to humour the upstart
Whilst deliberating how to bid him au revoir.

12 April

To remove Napoleon by appealing to his ego
The quintet instructs him to conquer Egypt for the glory of France.

If the upstart falls in battle, they muse
"Who's to say that'll be an unwelcome circumstance."

Napoleon is thrilled at the prospect of seizing Egypt
Judging an expedition under his command must surely succeed.
The quintet pledges to resource it
With the men and weaponry, the Général should need.

Raising thirty thousand infantry and three thousand cavalry
Signals the start of this far-reaching quest.
Alongside one hundred field and siege guns
The Egyptians will face the severest test.

The logistics for conveying this army are enormous
As twenty warships must escort three hundred transports or thereabout.
Yet, admirably, within ten weeks only
The expedition is ready to strike out.

20 May

News of the expedition quitting Toulon reaches Jervis
Whose fleet has been blockading Cadiz since Cape St Vincent.
The New World traders who convey this news
Have no knowledge of its destination or intent.

Keeping faith with Nelson despite his defeat at Santa Cruz,
Jervis asks him to lead a squadron to investigate.
Fellow admirals express their dismay
At the preferment of this headstrong initiate.

Nelson's mission has an inauspicious start with violent winds
Dismasting his flagship, *Vanguard*, prompting audible prayers.
The squadron's frigates sail direct to Gibraltar
Wrongly thinking *Vanguard* will follow to make repairs.

The absence of frigates hinders the squadron's effectiveness
By diminishing the coverage of good sea visibility.
Hunting the expedition will now rest
On the Navy's intelligence capability.

9 June
To please his countrymen, Napoleon sails first to Malta
Overcoming in two blood filled days the Knights of St John.
He loots the Order's historic treasures
And leaves behind an occupying garrison.

17 June

Elsewhere Nelson remains in dire need of sound intelligence

So he elects to sail to Naples, Britain's firm ally against France.
There, he entertains conflicting reports
Causing him to take the squadron on a merry dance.

Nelson heads directly for Alexandria at full speed
Calculating the expedition is en route to the Red Sea replete.
He swiftly overtakes Napoleon
Who's taking a circuitous journey, skirting Crete.

29 June

Failing to find the expedition at Alexandria
Devastates Nelson prompting self-doubt and an uncharacteristic rant.
He accepts the counsel of his captains
To widen the hunt by proceeding to The Levant.

As the squadron exits over the horizon to the east
The expedition, ironically, arrives en masse from the northwest.
Before nightfall, to Napoleon's joy
His transports make land without resistance or protest.

Eager not to delay executing his invasion plans,
Napoleon overwhelms the port to the sound of a restless drumbeat.
A forced march on Ciaro promptly follows
Across miles and miles of desert in summer heat.

Napoleon's sea commander, Amiral Brueys, takes shelter
Mooring his warships across Aboukir Bay in defensive formation.
And being surplus to requirements
He orders the transports back home for the duration.

19 July

Nelson's pursuit continues in vain beyond The Levant
Forcing him to dock at Syracuse to replenish declining supplies.
"The Devil's children have the Devil's luck."
Is the ignoble lament he utters to the skies.

28 July

Yet, God answers Nelson's prayers once the hunt resumes
When Greeks casting nets off Kalamata come to his aid.
They testify to seeing a great fleet
Southeast of Crete four weeks ago, fully lade.

Clasping his hands firmly in thankful praise, Nelson alters course
Confident that, on returning to Alexandria, the hunt will end.
He orders extra rapid-firing drills
In preparation of the engagement to impend.

1 August 1 P.M.

A breathless officer of the watch enters Nelson's cabin
"Sir, the enemy is in Aboukir Bay, moored in a line of battle."
"Hallelujah, we've found her
"Come, there's a great fleet to sink and no time to prattle."

7 P.M.

As the squadron's twelve seventy-four gunners enter the bay
There's less than an hour's light to keep the day from yawning.
Yet, despite a centuries-old convention
Nelson rejects delaying his attack till morning.

L'Orient exploding at the Battle of the Nile (Aboukir Bay)
1-3 August 1798

He notices that Brueys has striven to protect his van
By tucking it up against Bequier Island to the west of the bay.
And seeing a weakness with their moorings
Hastily starts formulating a tactical play.

If there's enough room for each Frenchman to swing on its anchor
There'll be sufficient space, Nelson concludes, to pass or anchor in its turn.
He rehearses the play with his captains
Holding to it despite expressions of concern.

Foley on *Goliath* rounds the leading Frenchman, *Guerrier*
Which, astern, *Zealous*, *Orion*, *Theseus* and *Audacious* emulate.
These Britons let loose furious broadsides
As they pass *Guerrier*, *Conquerant* and *Spartiate*.

Badly battered, *Conquerant* and *Spartiate* both fall silent
While *Guerrier* sinks, creating an opening through which the English can pour.
Vanguard, lying leeward of the French line,
Leads rapid bombardments targeting Brueys' core.

While observing with glee the potency of these bombardments
Nelson is struck on his forehead by a stray musket ball.
A flap of skin falls over his good eye

Prompting the witticism "Ah, it must be nightfall."
Capitaines in Brueys' core parade their patriotism
Including Thouars on *Tonnant*, whose limbs, one by one, are blown off.
From a wooden tub on his quarterdeck
He remains in command until his last spewing cough.

8 P.M.

Proving that courage alone can't repress inspired leadership
The first five Frenchmen, in turn, lower their flags to avoid going under.
With forty-two sutures in his forehead
From *Vangaurd's* poop deck, Nelson looks on in wonder.

Brueys' one-hundred-and-twenty-gun flagship, *Orient*,
Now makes her presence strongly felt, demasting eighth in line, *Bellerophon*.
Lovingly nicknamed "*Billy Ruffian*"
Her fellow Englishmen fear, with one more hit, she'll be gone.

Hallowell on *Swiftsure* hurriedly arrives to intervene
Selflessly interposing himself to draw *Orient's* splay.
The respite that *Billy Ruffian* gains
Allows her crew of five hundred to drift from harm's way.

As Hallowell anchors within yards of *Orient*
Ball, on *Alexander,* enters to strengthen the attack on Brueys' flagship.
Discharging broadsides consecutively
The two seventy-four-gun frigates let rip.

Flames start rising high into the air from *Orient's* gun decks
As drums of oil, her ill-disciplined crew left lying about, ignite.
Every Englishman's whose guns are within reach
Beset the flagship to prevent her taking flight.

Despite frantic attempts by *Orient's* crew to douse the flames
Extreme heat from the combusting oil beats them back again and again.
Brueys spots the magazine store smoking
"Que Dieu nous aide! Que Dieu nous aide!" is his last refrain.

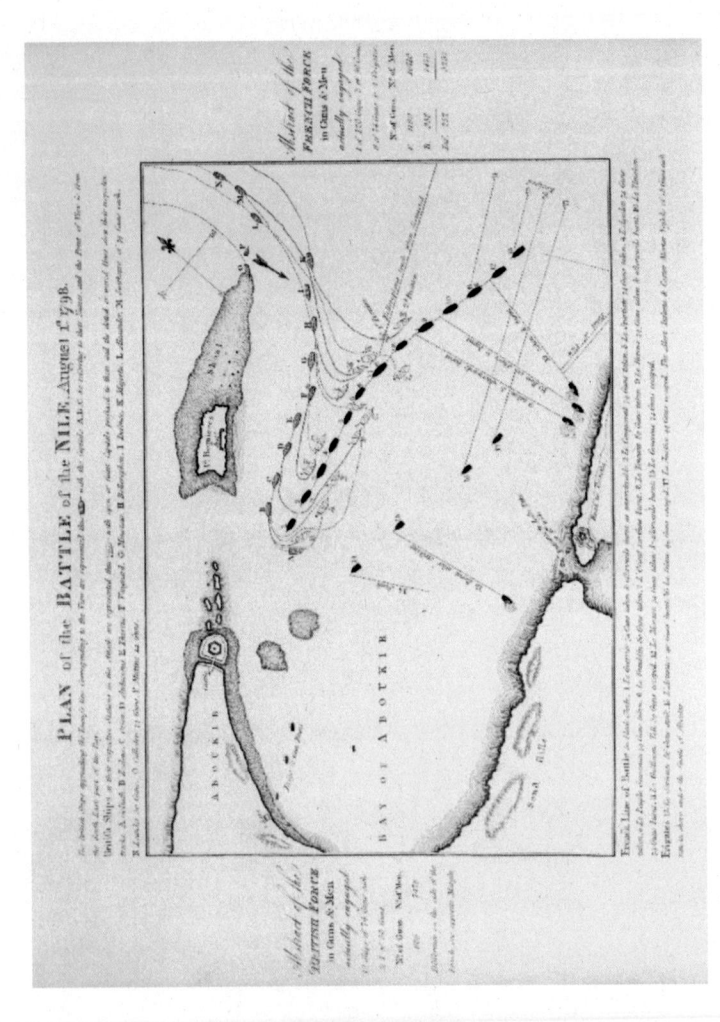

Ship positions and movements during the Battle of Nile.
1 August 1798

10 P.M.

A thunderous explosion issues from the magazine store
Prompting a brief cessation in hostilities while both sides stop and stare.
As burning bodies jump from *Orient*
On-lookers must confront the ugliness of warfare.

Nelson swiftly dispatches a boat to rescue survivors
To uphold a solemn naval tradition.
He knows honouring the enemy
Can't be sacrificed on the altar of ambition.

A salvo in *Vanguard's* direction restarts hostilities
To the despair of Amiral Villeneuve who's on board *Guillaume Tell*.
Commanding the rear of the French line
He recognises his powerlessness to repel.

Believing his objective must be to limit the rout,
Villeneuve instructs his three rearmost ships to sever their cables and flee.
Timoleon founders, running aground
But *Genereux* and *Guillaume Tell* both reach open sea.

Rather than countenance the English capturing their ship
Timoleon's crew sets her ablaze in an undisguised act of distain.
Her immolation brings to eleven

The Frenchmen wasted or seized in Nelson's coup de main.

2 August. 2 A.M.

The burning Frenchmen prevent the bay falling into darkness
Enabling Nelson to survey the trouncing none but he had foreseen.
As the engagement peters out, he claims
"Victory is not a name strong enough for this scene."

12 P.M.

Adhering to the courtesies afforded to the vanquished
Nelson invites the six surviving captains on-board *Vanguard* to dine.
Reciprocating his respectfulness
They attend in good humour and delight in the wine.

6 P.M.

The count of the French dead is over three thousand one hundred
To which must be added two thousand and seventy prisoners taken.
A humbling of this enormity
Will, surely, leave a nation's pride and prestige shaken.

Postscript

Nelson's dominant feeling after the battle is relief
Knowing that his reputation as a master tactician will revive.
Even his most grudging critics concede
His success will stand alone in the Navy's archive.

Brueys' defeat shatters confidence in the ruling quintet
Enabling ambitious Napoleon, within weeks, to take his chance.
Directing a brutal army-led coup
The Général proclaims himself First Consul of France.

Little Boney

Nelson's squadron celebrates its victory at the Battle of the Nile. 4 August 1798

How do you sink Little Boney's warships?
How do you sink Little Boney's warships?
How do you sink Little Boney's warships?
In the heat of battle!

Way hay watch them blow
Way hay watch them blow
Way hay watch them blow
In the heat of battle!

Launch an attack when they don't expect it
Launch an attack when they don't expect it
Launch an attack when they don't expect it
In the heat of battle!

Way hay watch them blow
Way hay watch them blow
Way hay watch them blow
In the heat of battle!

Sail around their van to get behind them

Sail around their van to get behind them
Sail around their van to get behind them
In the heat of battle.

Way hay watch them blow
Way hay watch them blow
Way hay watch them blow
In the heat of battle!

Approach their centre to get inside them
Approach their centre to get inside them
Approach their centre to get inside them
In the heat of battle.

Way hay watch them blow
Way hay watch them blow
Way hay watch them blow
In the heat of battle!

Catch them in the crossfire with rapid broadsides
Catch them in the crossfire with rapid broadsides
Catch them in the crossfire with rapid broadsides
In the heat of battle.

Way hay watch them blow
Way hay watch them blow
Way hay watch them blow
In the heat of battle!

That's how we sunk Little Boney's warships.

That's how we sunk Little Boney's warships.
That's how we sunk Little Boney's warships.
In the heat of battle!

Whinge

Nelson writes to Fanny following the Battle of the Nile.
18 August 1798

My Dearest Fanny

By the time this letter reaches your door
You'll know of my day of glory.
Believe all you read and more
It warrants a page in our island's story.

But a bullet tore flesh above my good eye
So I endure the hazards of war.
The surgeon's ugly stitches horrify
And the wound is damnably sore.

Worse, still, are the unremitting headaches
So painful, they stultify.
At night, alone, I get the shakes
It's quite enough to terrify.

Until Sunday, I thought I was done for
As Josiah will surely testify.
I'm praying my health will restore
When we sail to Naples, our ally.

The effort penning these few lines takes
You'd think I'd gone quite hoary.
I'm therefore reliant on fakes
To narrate my battle story.

So, for now, it's goodbye
With a plaintive sigh.

Yours ever
Horatio.

Re-Acquaintance

Sir William Hamilton

Nelson is reacquainted with Sir William and Lady Hamilton in Naples following the Battle of the Nile. 22 September 1798

Who's this happy-go-lucky Signora
Tying bunting to her residency's gate.
She's singing "Rule Britannia"
So has reason to celebrate.

She's a curious-looking Signora
With a fair complexion but rather fat.
She must be quite an extrovert
To wear such a fancy hat.

She's stepping onto the street
To hand out Union Flags.
Most takers are hapless urchins
Reduced to wearing rags.

An older distinguished Signor
Takes Signora by the arm.
Walking side by side
He radiates a diplomat's charm.

Signor escorts Signora to the port
Ahead of a massing crowd.
Friends approach lauding praise
On a nation that won't be cowed.

Half an hour later

On entering the port
Signora stops and stares.
Hundreds of pleasure craft are sailing
To greet a warship wanting repairs.

An aide de camp stands in uniform
By the quayside, taking charge.
Spotting Signor and Signora
He leads them to the royal barge.

Their Majesties welcome Signor
Who offers a respectful bow.
Signora attempts a curtsy
As low as her balance will allow.

Signora starts whooping for joy
As the barge casts off.
Her Majesty winces at the noise
Prompting courtiers to scoff.

Signor remains impassive
Preferring to let Signora be.
He knows there's no restraining
The excitement of a devotee.

Signora spies a telescope
Which she puts to her right eye.
Bringing the lens into focus

She emits an adoring sigh.

She leans over the side
To shoo the pleasure craft away.
There're impeding the barge's progress
And she can't abide the delay.

Half an hour later

Signora runs to the gangplank
As the warship comes along side.
Signor, too, joins the boarding party
Still repressing his inner pride.

A bandaged admiral salutes the king
In his broken Italian.
His Majesty honours this returning hero
Gifting a gold medallion.

Signora embraces the admiral
With questionable familiarity.
Amongst the disapproving courtiers
There's further cause for hilarity.

Birthday Party

Emma, Lady Hamilton

The Hamiltons host a lavish 40th birthday party for Nelson, British Embassy, Naples. 29 September 1798

I'm the hostess; please don't forget.
You mustn't do anything we'll both regret.
See Madam there; ask her to dance.
She'll never rebuff a sailor's advance.
Her husband's queer; that's the rumour.
She does well to keep a sense of humour.
Remove your hand! Not on my knee!
You're risking a scandal for all to see.
What about her? By the red chaise.
She's one of Naples easier lays.
But I like her; she can amuse
Recounting her years as Bonito's muse.
Horatio, will you behave?
You can't always have the women you crave.
Go charm the king, he needs cheering.
Thrill him with tales of your buccaneering.
He's in trouble, I'm afraid.
Word from London is France could invade.
Release my hand! I know your game.
I do your bidding or face public shame.
I'll surrender, but please don't mock.
I'll come to your bedroom at two o'clock.

Announcement

George III confers a peerage on Nelson. 6 October 1798

Whereas it is essential to Our Security and Welfare that Our Enemies should not molest Our Allies in the Mediterranean or elsewhere. And whereas France, worst of Our Foes, dispatched a great expedition to conquer the Land of the Pharaohs. And whereas Our loyal subject, Rear Admiral Sir Horatio Nelson Kt, Commanding our Blue Squadron, defeated Our Foe to Our Delight. And whereas We desire to honour Our loyal subject for his actions and feat, in thwarting at Aboukir Bay, Our Foe's designs and conceit. Now We declare and this day record that it is Our Royal will to award the dignity of a Baron to Our loyal subject and the heirs male of his bodily lawfully begotten; lest his service to Us be forgotten. And the name, title, and style conferred shall be Baron Nelson of the Nile.

George the Third, by the Grace of God, King of Great Britain, France, and Ireland, Defender of the Faith, and so forth.

Heartache

Fanny Nelson vents her anger. January 1801

I hear much, far too much, of Emma Hamilton
And it's all vile.
She's a mistress by profession
And my Horatio has fallen victim to her smile.
Or, rather, her dark arts and guile.

I see many, far too many, cartoons of their infidelity
And they'll all unflattering.
If that woman cared
She'd stop his reputation taking a battering.
But she's deaf to the chattering.

Horatio gets much, far too much, sympathy
And I'm the one maligned.
I didn't bear him a child
So, I'm compared to a baron hind.
Nothing could be more unkind.

I receive few, far too few, invitations now
And I'm becoming a recluse.
Hostesses entertain a whore
Who, in private, they traduce.

They've no earthly excuse!

Perhaps I'm indulging, too much, in self-pity?
But see how I'm treated.
I didn't ask for this
And it's my husband who's cheated.
Yet, it's my spirit that's been defeated.

Anger

Josiah articulates his anger over Nelson's infidelity.
February 1801

He's my father in all but name
Yet, how can I respect him?
His infidelity brings endless shame
Poor Mama, her life is grim.

He's been an excellent patron
And I have much to be thankful for.
But who can condone a liaison
That good society must abhor?

When arriving back in Dover
Every sailor knows what's expected.
It's goodbye to the rover
And marriage vows respected.

I doubt there'll be an outcry
Even though his conduct is vile.
Different standards seem to apply
When you're the "Hero of the Nile".

Newborn

Nelson writes to Lady Emma Hamilton on hearing of his daughter's birth. Torquay, February 1801

My darling Emma,
It's a great relief to know mother and baby are doing well. Waiting for tidings these last days has been hell. I had felt a foreboding since bidding you farewell.
You say our new-born has my likeness. If this were true, she can only impress. Yet, I do confess, don't all babies look the same?
There's no denying it will be a dreadful shame, but social mores demand that we disclaim being her parents despite the inevitable heart ache. For the baby's sake, the story we put about must be fake. I propose we say Willie and you fell upon a foundling in Vienna's Prater on a sightseeing tour. And to assure her wellbeing, Willie expressed a desire from which you could not demur. As an act of Christian charity, or if you wish to provoke hilarity, you could say noble piety, you brought her home to 23 Piccadilly. Even if this story raises eyebrows and to some, sounds silly, it should spare Willie. He doesn't deserve being met by a frown at every corner when going about town. Nor worse still, drawing sniggers as the deceived clown.

We should also say the baby was born in early December. Isn't that when you started back or was it late November? Whichever, please remember to maintain this pretence at little expense; engaging a wet nurse makes good sense. It's vital she's discreet, and Tommy Sweet recommends approaching Mrs Gibson of Little Titchfield Street.

There's no reason why I shouldn't be a godparent. I could visit the baby when otherwise I daren't. I'd have cover for going without appearing aberrant.

All turns on us acting in concert. So, whatever the hurt, we must never blurt; she's our own. We can't atone and her life would be well and truly thrown. She'd never live down the disgrace. You, too, must acknowledge that's the case. No respectable man would consider making her a proposal of marriage. There'd be no ceremony with horse and carriage. Only remarks designed to disparage, even though the father sits in the House of Peers.

These, my beloved Emma, are my well-founded fears, from which she must safeguarded all her years. Please say you agree.

I remain, as always, your obedient devotee.

Nelson & Brontë

Battle of Copenhagen

Title Battle of Copenhagen viewed from a Danish floating battery 2 April 1801

Nelson disobeys his commander in battle. April 1801

The most celebrated act of disobedience
In Royal Navy history
Happened at the Battle of Copenhagen
When Lord Nelson was pushing for victory.

As second-in-command,
Nelson raised a telescope to his blind eye,
And joked, "I really do not see the signal."
To excuse his failure to comply.

The signal from first-in-command, Sir Hyde Parker
Ordered Nelson to break off his attack,
But Nelson, who suspected Parker lacked courage,
Had no intention of holding back.

Although not at war with Denmark or Sweden,
Britain had dispatched a fleet to this expanse,
To deter these two Baltic states
Aligning themselves with Napoleonic France.

On the eighteenth of March, in swirling snow,
Parker reached the tip of Jutland,
And, after navigating down the Kattegat,
Dispatched an ultimatum by hand.

The terms unsettled the Danish Court
Sending Crown Prince Frederick into a huff,

And, after five days of deliberation,
He answered Parker with a firm rebuff.

Parker entered the Oresund on the thirteenth
With full arsenals and compliments of men,
And, in sight of Copenhagen harbour,
Anchored off Isle of Hven.

Whilst judging Nelson to be irresponsible,
Parker valued him as a tactician,
So asked him to devise a battle plan
To deliver on the mission.

Nelson found the harbour well protected,
By the shoal of Middle Ground,
Plus heavy guns at Trekroner Fort,
And demasted warships tightly bound.

Nelson counted nineteen such warships
In King's Channel, stretching over a mile
From the fort in the north
To the east of Amager Isle.

Nelson proposed to his squadron
A battle plan, he thought, Parker might veto,
Of entering King's Channel from the southeast
And anchoring opposite each foe.

Nelson also had in mind a land assault
To knock out the canons at the fort,

Using a company of well-trained marines
With three frigates in support.

To assist his masters navigate Middle Ground
Nelson spent hours in a flat-bottomed boat
Plotting a route where buoys should go
To keep the squadron afloat.

Nelson's captains dined on his flagship, *Elephant*,
After plotting finished on the thirty-first,
When heavy bets were laid
On the number of ships, they'd worst.

At sunrise on the second of April
Parker, who had misgivings, instructed
Nelson to execute the battle plan
He had so painstakingly constructed.

Lead by Captain Murray on *Edgar*,
Nelson's twelve ships of the line
Plus assorted frigates and bomb-ketches,
Set off in weather oddly benign.

Although they followed Nelson's route
Agamemnon, *Russell* and *Bollona* ran aground
So badly weakening the line's northern end,
It hurriedly had to be switched around.

As the line couldn't respond to salvos
Until anchored in formation,

Polyphemus sustained heavy damage
Adding to Nelson's frustration.

But once the line entered King's Channel,
Each warship brought its fire power to bear,
Discharging at a range of two hundred yards
Broadsides rapidly into the air.

At a rate of one every forty seconds,
Nelson hoped to solicit a quick submission,
But the Danes responded tenaciously
Initiating a war of attrition.

Crowds of Copenhageners took to rooftops
To witness the drama unfold,
And observing the initial exchanges,
Expected the defences to hold.

By half past one, Parker, too, began to doubt
Whether continuing made sense,
And, on seeing *Elephant's* mainmast hit,
Suffered a crisis of confidence.

Nelson ignored Parker's signal to disengage
Convinced his battle plan would prevail,
And turning to his Flag Captain, Foley,
Declared, "This is no time for one's nerve to fail."

Raising his telescope to his eye patch
He faced Parker's flagship, *London*, wearing a smile,

Adding, "I've only one eye."
"So I can be blind once in a while."

Besides Captain Riou on *Amazon*
Whose assault on the fort was cursed,
Every captain disobeyed Parker
Putting their devotion to Nelson first.

Over the next hour and a quarter
The squadron's dogged persistence
In loosing rapid broadsides,
Greatly weakened the Danes' resistance.

As gun smoke blackened the sky,
And fireballs reduced their ships to wrecks,
Watching crowds started to weary
Of the battle's grimmer effects.

Overwhelmed by a quarter past three,
Danish captains began to tire,
And after several struck their colours
Nelson offered a ceasefire.

Acceptance of the offer
Ended the battle at a quarter to four,
Leaving both sides to attend to their wounded
And bury those no more.

Of the Danes' nineteen ships in King's Channel
The flagship, *Danneborg*, burned,

Eleven were seized for their prize
And one overturned.

The following evening, Nelson attended
A banquet hosted by Prince Frederick,
And, in toasting the bravery of the Danish forces,
Exhibited a skill to politic.

The good impression Nelson made
Facilitated the signing of an accord
Reversing France's influence in the Baltic,
An outcome the Admiralty must applaud.

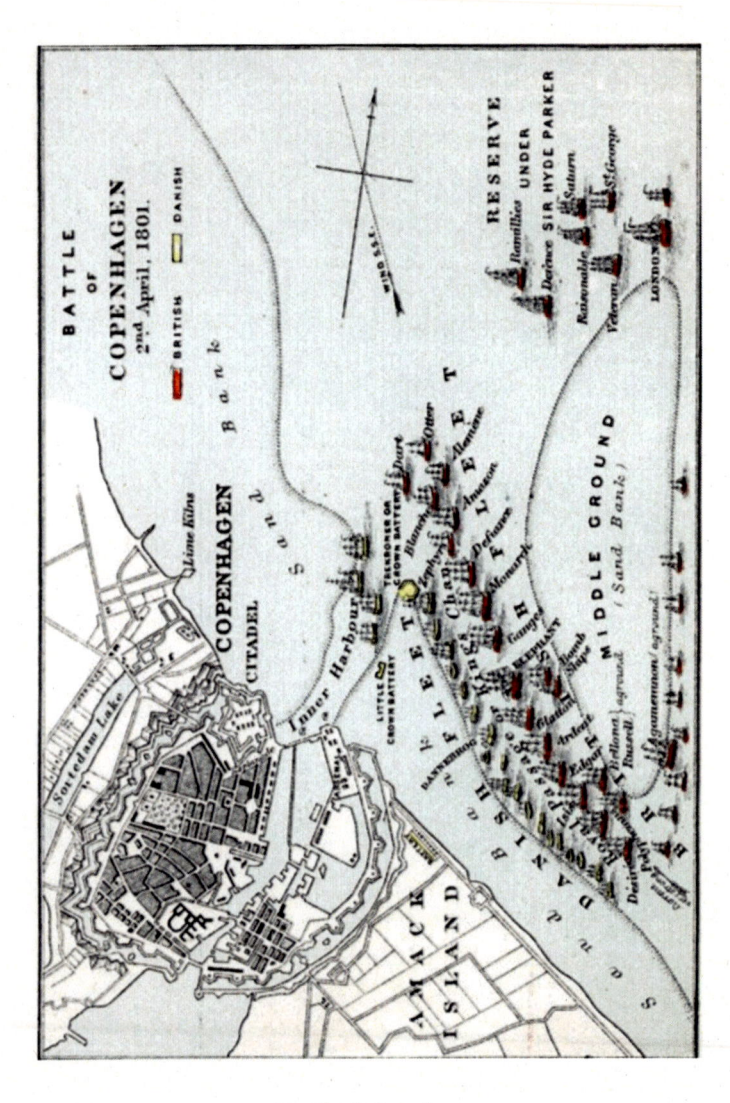

Battle of Copenhagen

Gun-Captain

A gun-captain on board *HMS Defiance* instructs a new powder monkey. 2 April 1801

He'd better be spunky.
Our new powder monkey!
Ah, there you are.
Welcome to the best gun crew by far.
Been hiding behind the gunwale?
Well, it's too late now to bail.
Big guns in the channel ahead lie in wait.
They'll hold our fete.
You're what, twelve, thirteen and tough?
Good, as things will get bloody rough.
We'll be assigned a Dane to blow
So, on deck, it'll be all go.
Now, boy.
This canon here; she's no toy!
She needs gunpowder – lots of it
Every time she's lit.
That's your task.
Topping up each flask
With black stuff from the magazine store
For Bob, there, to pour.
So, when I shout, you come running

Otherwise, I'll come gunning.
For you, that is.
Got it?

Bitterness
(With Acknowledgements to Roland Orzabal)

Nelson is warned by his father, Rev. Edmund Nelson, why he should not resent a lack of official recognition after the Battle of Copenhagen. August 1801

No good comes of bitterness
Nothing's won, nothing son
Face descent which our Lord will shun
Damaged soul, damaged soul
Hell will surely wish to welcome you
Honoured guest, honoured guest
Mark my words before it's too late
Choose your fate, choose your fate.

And I'd find it self-defeating; I'd find it rather odd
If the slight to your brothers turned you from the word of God.
I don't doubt what's due to them; they're known for their grit
When rulers have mean spirits, it's a very very
Harsh world, harsh world.

Scripture teaches not to crave earthly honours

No true worth, no true worth
Remember who inherits the Earth
Will you listen, will you listen?
Unfortunate their treatment of you
No earldom, no earldom
First Sea Lord wrote you deserve it
You shouldn't quit, you shouldn't quit.

And I'd find it self-defeating; I'd find it rather odd
If the slights you've mentioned turned you from the word of God
A hero to the Navy, you're mobbed in the streets
When left to common people, it's a very very
Fine world, fine world.

The King Confides

George III confides in Queen Charlotte. November 1801

Of course, I deplore his infidelity
Although half our family has strayed.
But presenting the wife at court,
Why, I'm forced to condone the charade.

It's his lack of discretion I object to,
Escorting the mistress all over town.
And the husband, I'm told, is complicit,
Yes, my dear, you may well frown.

He may be feted wherever he goes
But that's the lower classes for you.
They've always loved their sailors
And tales of derring-do.

I know how indebted we are to him
William Henry never lets me forget.
But raising him to a viscount
That's something I now regret.

There's talk of bastard daughter,

Canterbury and York think it's true.
York wants him excommunicated
And Canterbury run through.

Hiatus

Nelson takes an extended leave from active duty.
October 1801 – May 1803

Late 1801

The signing of the Treaty of Amiens
Ushered an uneasy year-long peace
Between Britain and Napoleonic France
Enabling the Admiralty to release
Ships protecting His Majesty's domain
Until required for a future campaign.

So it was that Horatio came to take
Extended leave from the active duty
To engage openly in a *ménage à trois*
With the lusty, voluptuous beauty
Emma Hamilton and her ageing husband
Vexing polite society throughout the land.

Quite indifferent to all adverse comment
Horatio found domestic pleasure
He hadn't experienced for many years
So much so, he used his amassed treasure
To acquire near Twickenham a country pile

Where he could greet guests in sumptuous style.

Only one-hour's ride from the Admiralty
Merton House was conveniently placed
Allowing Horatio to stay in touch
With the 'Band of Brothers' he embraced
Who judged like him keeping the island race sweet
Rested on the inventiveness of her fleet.

Horatio's acquisition of Merton House
Helped heal the rift with his ailing Pop
Who had stayed loyal to his daughter-in-law
(Despite his son's rise to the top)
With Emma assuaging Pop's lingering qualms
By making full use of her feminine charms.

1802

The rapprochement between father and son
Couldn't have come at a better time
As within the year, Pop had passed away
Leaving Horatio to recall Pop's rhyme:
"Don't be found despairing in moments of doubt
Nor wanting courage to turnabout."

The customary period of mourning
Gave way to a desire to complete
An extensive tour of the West Country
To include Sir William's family seat
Now heavily mortgaged to pay for
His years in Sicily as ambassador.

Every town Horatio entered was eager
To mark the presence of their hero
By arranging civic banquets
Fetes and even the odd cattle show
Where cheering crowds would loudly sing
'Rule Britannia' and 'God save the King'.

Early 1803

The travelling *ménage's* tour ended abruptly
When news reached Jervis of Boney's scheme
To seize control of the English Channel
As a prelude to fulfilling his dream
Of sacking the one nation whose prominence
Impeded his goal of world dominance.

Jervis recalled Horatio in haste
To help him organise and pursue
The defence of the realm against invasion
By the only sure means they both knew:
Naval mastery over their rival
To defer a crossing and hence survival.

On quitting Melton House for active duty
Emma's long, passionate parting kiss
Brought to a close, Horatio's year of bliss.

Not Tonight, Josephine

Josephine interrupts Napoleon's preparations to invade England. November 1804

Not tonight, Josephine
I'm busy, can't you see?
I've no time to argue
So please, let me be.

If you're bored, read a book
Just spare us all a hissy fit.
You're Empress of France
Kindly act like it.

Ouch, that damn well hurt
And it's vintage champagne.
Perhaps you'll learn respect
If you feel this cane?

Are you quite finished?
You've keeping a guest waiting.
It's Spain's ambassador
Who'll now require placating.

He's here to receive my grand plan

To land on English soil.
It's quite ingenious,
So will be hard to foil.

They're a nation of shopkeepers
I'm restless to tame.
Until I humble England
I won't achieve world fame.

Tomorrow, I'll treat you
How about Opera-comique?
But only if you leave
Without another squeak.

Spain's Assent

Spain's ambassador responds to Napoleon's grand plan for invading Britain. November 1804

The plan is worthy of your reputation
And plainly warrants our participation.
First Secretary Godoy will assent,
Of this, I am quite confident.

He, in particular, is feeling the heat
Of last October's assault on our treasure fleet.
At court, your plan should helpfully abate,
Rash demands to retaliate.

We will contribute fifteen ships of good size
To demonstrate our commitment to this enterprise.
Together, our combined force will surely be
The strongest ever put to sea.

Before landing troops at Romney beach,
Indeed, seize their West Indies' possessions in our reach.
Inciting panic by such humbling blows
Must erode their will to oppose.

I pray invasion offers a return home
To the welcoming arms of our church in Rome.
Righting Henry Tudor's historic wrong
Will, I'm sure, be extolled in song.

Pitt's Anguish

Prime Minister William Pitt (The Younger) expresses his anguish to his private secretary following intelligence of a renewed alliance between France and Spain to invade Britain. January 1805

If our spies report correctly
Spain will be declaring war directly.
And there's every chance
She'll willingly collude with France.
And she'll need little persuasion
To spearhead an invasion.
With two armies versus one
Who's to say we won't be undone.

As Prime Minister, I recoil
At the thought of our beloved island in turmoil.
Every pupil learns at school
Not since William the Conqueror's rule,
Have unfriendly troops landed here.
Ten sixty-six was the year.
A landing would deal a psychological blow
Like the failed walls of Jericho.

Even when domestic currents swirl

And election colours unfurl,
There's something special about our Island race
As if we live in a state of grace.
Whatever the abuse hurled
We must be a force for good in the world.
Or we are naught.
So, my father taught.

I had an audience with the king;
He fears losing everything.
I, too, felt numb
Just thinking how they'll come.
To steady his Majesty's nerves
I promised enlisting reserves.
And taking courage from the Lionheart
To see off the monster Bonaparte.

If we're occupied
My end will be undignified.
Like the king and queen
I'll have an appointment with Madam Guillotine.
Of course, providence could dictate
I be spared this fate.
But who's the Englishman I should call
Who's got the wit to save us all?

Worse for Wear Sailor
(With Acknowledgments to Jimmy Webb)

Nelson addresses his fellow officers on taking command of the Mediterranean fleet. September 1805

I am a sailor for my country
And I sail the high seas
Searching in the storms for a rival fleet to squeeze
I best them firing at close quarters
I board many for their prize
And this worse for wear sailor
Has yet to capsize.

I know I share your huge frustration
But peace doesn't stand a hope;
And if France and Spain come at us
This squadron's trained to cope.
And I love you, band of brothers
And I'll serve you to the last;
And this worse for wear sailor
Knows the dye is cast.

Deliverance

Viscount Horatio Nelson before the Battle of Trafalgar 21 October 1805

Battle of Trafalgar, off the south-west coast of Spain.
21 October 1805

Context

On much, if not most, of continental Europe
France has become the dominant political power,
As her army ruler, Napoleon Bonaparte,
Forces opponents on the battlefield to cower.

England, alone, with her doughty Royal Navy
Presents an embarrassing obstacle to Boney's quest,
Of greatly enhancing France's global influence,
By blockading her naval ports of Toulon and Brest.

In his firm resolve to remove this obstacle,
Boney vows to invade England before the year's over,
But he knows he must wrest control of The Channel,
If *la grande armée* is to land safely near Dover.

Although plainly critical to an invasion,
Morale within France's navy is not what it's been,
As febrile politics in the ruling *Consulat*
Sends talented officers to *La Guillotine*.

England, in contrast, boasts a corps of officers
Whose enthusiasm for Nelson's derring-do
Endows her navy with a 'Band of Brothers'
Courageous, resourceful and battle hardened too.

On learning of Boney's appointment of Villeneuve
To take command of France's Mediterranean fleet,
The Bothers recall his cowardly flight at the Nile,
Inducing prolonged hilarity full of conceit.

Boney's strategy endorsed by his ally, Spain,
Has their fleets in Cadiz and the Mediterranean
Breaking through the Royal Navy's tight blockades,
Then combining en route to the Caribbean.

The Combined fleet will return under Villeneuve
To aid besieged ships at Brest break the last blockade,
Before clearing The Channel of the Royal Navy
To ensure *la grande armée* can safely be conveyed.

Taking command of the blockade off Toulon,
Nelson decides to lure Villeneuve into leaving port,
By visibly loosening their existing presence,
Confident emerging ships will be caught.

March

Sensing his chance to implement Boney's strategy,
Villeneuve (as Nelson had hoped) bids for open water,
And luckily for him, his ships evade capture
When Nelson's lurkers scatter widely in a snorter.

After regrouping, Nelson sails east in pursuit,
Yet, in going east, his judgment again goes awry,
As Villeneuve sails west through the Strait of Gibraltar

Intending to rendezvous with his Spanish ally.

Not until he arrives at Alexandria
Does a red-faced Nelson acknowledge he's made a mistake,
And, if he's to engage the Combined fleet in battle,
Crossing the North Atlantic is the course he must take.

June

Embarrassment turns to audible frustration
When Villeneuve, who's restocking in Martinique,
Decides to sail home just as Nelson reaches Antigua,
Thus prolonging their criss-crossing game of hide and seek.

Adhering to Boney's invasion strategy,
Villeneuve navigates for Brest to break the blockade there,
But encounters an English squadron led by Calder
Off the north-western tip of Spain, near Cape Finistere.

In the ensuing battle, cut short by nightfall,
Calder's inferior squadron captures two Spanish ships,
Prompting Villeneuve to retreat to nearby Ferrol
To Boney's exasperation and withering quips.

Villeneuve receives terse instructions from Boney
Demanding compliance with his invasion strategy,
To reinforce the Combined fleet by relieving Brest

Ahead of clearing The Channel for *la grande armée*.

August

Villeneuve sails the Combined fleet towards Cadiz
Fully cognisant, he's risking Boney's severe reprove,
And all because he feels increasingly despondent
At the Royal Navy observing his every move.

Nelson returns to England for a welcome break,
And, despite his recent setbacks, is met with praise,
But news of Villeneuve entering Cadiz Harbour
Shortens his leave ashore to twenty-five days.

September

Nelson consults Prime Minister Pitt and the king
Then bids an affectionate farewell to Emma, his favourite,
And Horatia, their love child
Before rejoining *Victory* renewed and fighting fit.

Cornwallis, who's patrolling the English Channel,
Reckons twenty ships under his command should be detached,
To bolster Calder's squadron stalking the Combined fleet,
Even if this hazards leaving his patrol ill-matched.

The detachment reaches Calder before Nelson

Who, on arriving, hosts the captains of the fleet,
To articulate his radical battle tactic
For securing Villeneuve's comprehensive defeat.

Nelson has at his disposal
Three first, four second and twenty third rates,
Plus three lesser gunships earmarked for early retirement,
And four frigates and two schooners – in differing states.

In contrast, Villeneuve's estimable line-up
Boasts three of the four most powerful first rates ever made,
Plus, twenty-nine third rates and five frigates,
Affording him far superior cannonade.

Nelson abandons tactical orthodoxy,
Knowing, in all likelihood, he'll come horribly undone
If the two fleets face each other broadside in a line
With each ship committing to a one-on-one.

He proposes cutting Villeneuve's line in three
By attacking at right angles in two parallel rows,
Near the centre and towards the tail end,
Then bombarding the middle third with crippling blows.

His preference is to cut Villeneuve's centre
Immediately in front of flagship, *Bucentaure*,

So other isolated ships can't see her signals
As they attempt to reform in the battle's roar.

The inherent risk in Nelson's tactic,
Of exposing his lead ships advancing on Villeneuve's line
To broadsides aimed at their bows without means of defence,
Is accepted by the Brothers without whinge or whine.

Nelson intends to take the brunt of these broadsides
Jointly with Collingwood, his deputy and faithful friend,
With each fronting an advancing row,
Nelson the centre, and Collingwood the tail-end.

Drawing on past engagements to help the Brothers,
Nelson asks them to paint their ships with yellow and black check,
So, through the bellowing gun-power smoke of battle,
They'll discern the enemy from their command deck.

October

Boney, who's still sore from Villeneuve's defiance,
Orders him to quit Cadiz as soon as events permit,
And sail the Combined fleet eastwards to Cartagena
Where seven more Spaniards are ready to commit.

Villeneuve holds a war council on board *Bucentaure*
Only to find his captains angrily disagreeing,
Over whether to obey Boney's orders,
With most against (at least) for the time being.

Villeneuve had advocated for staying put,
Yet, the very next day, he abruptly changes his view,
On hearing of his dismissal by the *Consulat*
With handover to occur within a week or two.

To lessen the humiliation, he'll suffer
Once news of his dismissal is known by the world at large,
Villeneuve resolves to sail immediately
To prevent his successor, Rosily, taking charge.

The Combined fleet heads for the Straits of Gibraltar
But, with visibility good and winds turning light,
Villeneuve knows there's no avoiding the English fleet
So, he must hurriedly deploy for the coming fight.

The fall of Nelson on the quarterdeck of HMS Victory *at the Battle of Trafalgar. 21 October 1805*

21 October

Dawn

Villeneuve is forming his single battle line
When he spots the English about twenty miles away,
Approaching from northwest of Cape Trafalgar
He judges hostilities must commence by midday.

11 A.M.

With the two fleets almost in range of each other,
Villeneuve's unevenly spaced line five miles in length,
Faces Nelson's well-disciplined parallel rows,
Thus pitting strategy against superior strength.

Whilst the English – to a man – knows what's at stake,
Nelson signals his ships to dispel any lagging fears,
"England expects every man will do his duty",
Knowing this'll provoke animated cheers.

Practically at right angles to the Combined fleet,
Nelson, who's leading the windward row, feints changing tack
Towards the front of Villeneuve's line, to mislead,
Before reverting to the pre-planned point of attack.

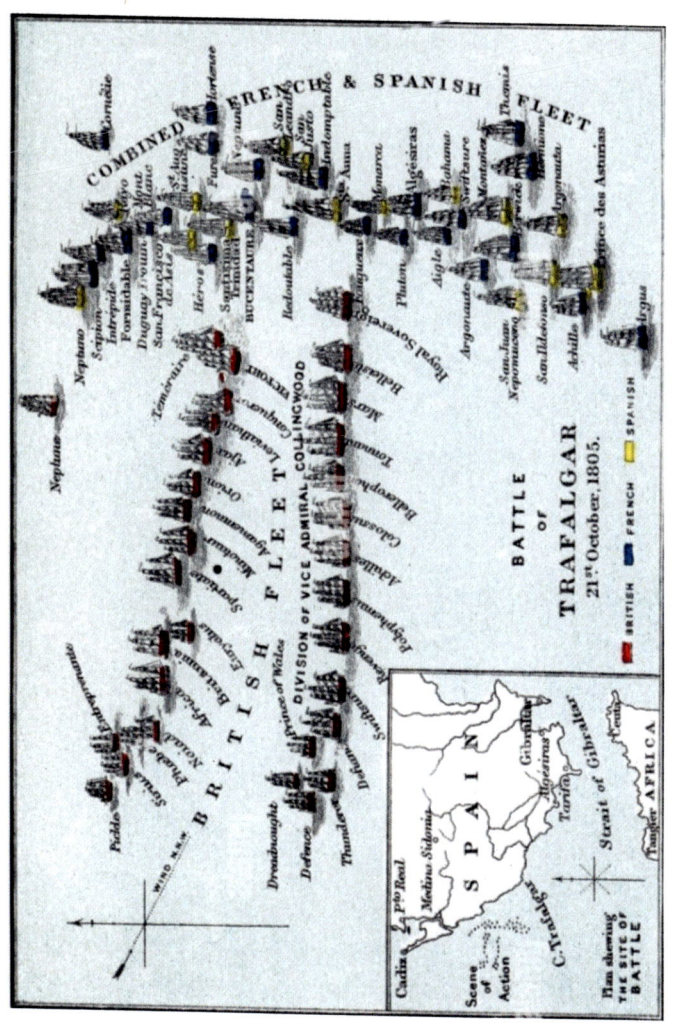

The British fleet breaking through the French and Spanish line.
21 October 1805 line

Noon

Villeneuve, in response, signals *"engage the enemy"*
Whereupon *Fougueux* fires trial shots at the leeward row,
Missing Collingwood's ship, *Royal Sovereign*,
As she advances, with all sails out, on the foe.

As *Royal Sovereign* closes, she comes under sustained fire
From *Fougueux*, *San Justo*, *San Leandro* and *Indomptable*,
Before breaking the line astern of *Santa Ana*
And discharging a well-aimed broadside at her.

Nelson, watching from on-board Victory, applauds
"See how that noble Collingwood carries his ship to win!"
Only to see *L'Aigle*, *Achille*, *Neptune* and *Fougueux*
Take aim at *Belleisle*, who's next behind *Royal Sovereign*.

These four quickly dismast *Belleisle*, crippling her
Yet, despite sails and rigging severely blinding her guns,
Under Captain Hargood, she keeps flying her flag
Gamely, for forty-five minutes, until relief comes.

Victory, too, suffers greatly whilst advancing,
As salvos from *Santísima Trinidad* and *Héros*
Blow her steering wheel killing many,
But morale holds despite this grievous loss.

12:45 P.M.

By ably steering her tiller from below decks
Victory's resourceful Captain Hardy maintains his course,
Breaking the line near Villeneuve's flagship, *Bucentaure*,
Then firing a broadside through her stern with no remorse.

Hardy decides against capturing *Bucentaure*
Opting to leave this task to others in the windward row,
So he can train his guns on nearby *Redoubtable*
In the hope of delivering another heavy blow.

As *Victory* and *Redoubtable* touch locking masts,
Nelson is hit by a stray musket bullet made of lead,
Cracking his spine at the sixth and seventh vertebrae,
Making him to cry in pain: *"They've succeeded; I'm dead."*

While stretcher bearers swiftly take Nelson below
Hardy, who's facing an imminent boarding attack,
Calls his gunners on deck for close combat
But grenades hurled from *Redoubtable* force them back.

Temeraire, second in the windward row,
To immense English relief, comes to *Victory's* rescue,
By approaching *Redoubtable* from the starboard bow
And bombarding to decimation her exposed crew.

13.55 P.M.

Left with only ninety-nine able-bodied men
From a compliment of six hundred and forty-two,
Redoubtable's Captain Lucas, himself badly maimed,
Strikes her colours conceding nothing less will do.

Temeraire now moves to isolate *Bucentaure*
Encouraging *Neptune*, *Leviathan* and *Conqueror*,
Who are lying third, fourth and fifth in the windward row,
To act in concert in overwhelming her.

Villeneuve turns ashen watching from *Bucentaure's* poop deck
As his crew tries vainly to repel the English trio,
But, beset by mounting loss of life, he surrenders
Yielding the flagship to *Conqueror's* Captain Pellow.

2:30 P.M.

More of the Brothers start entering the battle
Triggering a succession of close one-on-one contests.
Half hidden by bellowing smoke,
They loose rapid broadsides eager for conquests.

The Brothers' greater experience
And their better-trained gunners, who provide more clout,
Gradually, tells in the one-on-one contests
Offering Nelson solace as he slowly bleeds out.

Villeneuve's hitherto inactive van
Makes a token showing before beating a quick retreat,
Exposing themselves to taunts of cowardice
For condemning their centre and rear to sure defeat.

4:30 P.M.

Hardy scrambles below to report a triumph.
Only to hear Nelson murmur with his last breath,
"Thank God I have done my duty",
Leaving him, teary-eyed, to mourn the admiral's death.

The Brothers capture twenty-two ships in total
Without so much as losing a single one of their own,
And, visualising his next audience with Boney,
Villeneuve weighs what he can say or do to atone.

Aftermath

But there's no placating Boney's displeasure,
Who murders Villeneuve for not subduing Albion,
Whereas King George leads his people's tributes to Nelson,
Ordering a state funeral for their champion.

The Royal Navy's mastery at Trafalgar
Ends for a century all invasion threats,
Enabling England through courage and wit to transform

Into "*the Empire on which the sun never sets*".

Last Words

Nelson's dying words in HMS Victory's cockpit. 21 October 1805

Your face says it all, Beatty.
There's nothing you can do.
My back is shot through.
My legs are numb.
I know my time has come.

Are you listening, Beatty?
Go treat those you can save.
Leave this wretched knave.
You're wasted here.
And, no, don't shed a tear.

Where's Hardy, find Hardy.
Try the quarterdeck first.
I must know who's come off worst.
Have I secured His Majesty's reign?
Would be cruel, if my sacrifice were in vain.

Sit Hardy, speak Hardy.
Has my plan won the day?
Well, out with it – yea or nay.
[Hardy nods]

The Lord be praised in all his glory!
There'll be more chapters to our island's story.

Demand an audience with the king, Hardy.
To plead for Lady Hamilton on my behalf.
Emma mustn't face the tipstaff.
She has no independent means.
Not a row of beans.

If Pitt wishes to honour my deeds, Hardy.
If the nation owes me a debt of gratitude.
Let the king put aside his feud.
Grant Emma an annuity.
Then let her be.

Come closer, Hardy, closer.
I've done my duty.
Witnessed love, glory and inner beauty.
[*Nelson looks left*]
I'm a Christian, a man of faith!
I don't fear you, approaching wraith!

Kiss me, Hardy, kiss me.
Here, on my forehead.
I feel the cold of the nearly dead.
Take my hand; I'll not die alone.
God, for all my sins, I atone.

Reflections
(To Be Sung to 'Veni Emmanuel')

A nation in mourning reflects on Nelson's life.
November 1805

Our son, our son, Horatio
No saint, but died a true hero,
Whose legacy we shan't forget
In saving England when beset.
Honour! Honour! Horatio
Deliverer against a tyrant foe.

Our son, born to sweet genteel poor,
Whose cleric father would implore,
'Follow the Holy Writ's teaching
To make life's purpose far-reaching'.
Honour! Honour! Horatio
Deliverer against a tyrant foe.

Our son, at school was all listful,
Yet, sea-dog yarns turned him wistful.
Dire cast, at thirteen he enrolled,
Romanticism had taken hold.
Honour! Honour! Horatio
Deliverer against a tyrant foe.

Our son, lowly, gumptious coxswain
Lusted for an active campaign.
So eager was he to impress
Through valour and mental quickness.
Honour! Honour! Horatio
Deliverer against a tyrant foe.

Our son, peers would frankly confess
'Tis around him we'd coalesce'.
Charisma and tactical gift
Made his ascent to captain swift.
Honour! Honour! Horatio
Deliverer against a tyrant foe.

Our son, often risked court martial,
As, in battle, he'd be partial,
To defying his commander
Who, in private, he'd slander.
Honour! Honour! Horatio
Deliverer against a tyrant foe.

Our son, observed the naval code,
Exemplified by respect owed
To rivals beaten in warfare
By treating their captured with care.
Honour! Honour! Horatio
Deliverer against a tyrant foe.

Our son, became celebrity

Despite known infidelity.
Applause for his derring-do wins
Muted censure of private sins.
Honour! Honour! Horatio
Deliverer against a tyrant foe.

Our son, when raised to admiral
Faced jibes of 'reckless know-it-all',
For spurning received ways of war,
'Antics' now glorified in lore.
Honour! Honour! Horatio
Deliverer against a tyrant foe.

Our son, inspired loyalty
Second only to royalty.
By putting himself in harm's way
His captains were loathed to gainsay.
Honour! Honour! Horatio
Deliverer against a tyrant foe.

Our son, suffered bad maimings twice,
To him, a modest sacrifice
For serving countrymen and king
By drawing Napoleon's sting.
Honour! Honour! Horatio
Deliverer against a tyrant foe.

Our son, after a failed attack
Agonised before bouncing back.
The Naval Lords didn't waver

Confident they'd found their saviour.
Honour! Honour! Horatio
Deliverer against a tyrant foe.

Our son, in the decisive fight,
Used intellect to dumbfound might.
So complete was the victory,
None threatened for a century.
Honour! Honour! Horatio
Deliverer against a tyrant foe.

Our son, had a shortened story,
Killed in his moment of glory.
A people reduced to sadness
Reflect on his feats with gladness.
Honour! Honour! Horatio
Deliverer against a tyrant foe.

Lying in State

Rear Admiral Cuthbert Collingwood

Nelson's friend and deputy at the Battle of Trafalgar, Cuthbert Collingwood, attends Nelson's lying in state at the Royal Hospital for Seaman, Greenwich. 7 January 1806

A colleague finds an empty chair
Close to where mourners pause,
And bow their heads in deep respect
To a hero of the nation's cause.
From York to Haverfordwest
They come sporting Sunday best.

I am here, too, Horatio
To say a final farewell,
And pray you ascend to heaven
To rest with our Lord, Emmanuel.
You richly deserve this reward
Though you will, I fear, soon get bored.

George will miss Wednesday's service
Claiming the king is to blame
In refusing to waive protocol,
But that is not the only shame.
Fanny said 'No' in full glare,
So, Emma, too, will not be there.

I wish in this world of ours
We were less willing to vent,
But showed more generosity

And selflessness equal to the moment.
I will fetch Emma after-hours
Even if the Bishop glowers.

In seventy-seven, it was
When we met on *Lowestoffe,*
Both newly posted lieutenants,
And neither the customary toff.
Even then, you would make us laugh
Mocking officers, you thought daft.

I never took your mockery
As impatience of an upstart,
But desire to wrest power
From our adversary, Bonaparte.
You understood better than most,
His threat to invade was no boast.

I had better not reminisce
In case we both start cringing
At our pranks in the early days
When no chap's beard was safe from singeing.
We signed up though, when war arrived
For tough deployments and survived.

Though your uncle was comptroller,
To your enduring credit,
You remained anxious to ensure
Each promotion was gained on merit.
Our band of brothers will attest,
No commander more impressed.

I wager you chuckled a lot
At the recounting in print
Of our triumph at Trafalgar
In rose-coloured patriotic tint.
Details of how you lay there dead
Ensured inside pages were well-read.

The ups and downs of service life
Forged a friendship to treasure,
And, over some twenty-eight years,
We laughed and cried in equal measure.
In our job, we know loss and pain,
Yet, this one is hard to explain.

In case you did not realise,
I fulfilled my allotted task,
So, you can take comfort knowing
Your box is wood from *L'Orient's* mask.
Although I vowed to keep tight-lipped,
You are destined for St. Paul's crypt.

Jervis has arrived, Horatio,
I should go to say hello.

Horatia Nelson kneeling before her father's (imaginary) tomb

Toast to the Royal Navy

Author's personal tribute.

To his Britannic Majesty's Navy, pride and joy of our nation,
By this oath, I swear eternal allegiance to thee.
Who, since the glorious days of Effingham and our beloved Drake,
Have never faltered in the wake,
Of foreign powers with covetous eyes,
Plotting and intriguing our demise.

To his Britannic Majesty's Navy, whose strength comes from England's noble oak,
By this pledge, with courage shall I serve thee.
Who, since the glorious days of Vanguard, and our beloved Ark Royal
Has never failed to foil,
Threats to our Channel coast.
Our liberty and freedom is the toast.

Si vis pacem, pare bellum
If you wish for peace, prepare for war.

To all would-be heroes:
"Don't be found despairing in moments of doubt
Nor wanting courage to turnabout."

Sir Thomas Hardy, Vice Admiral of the Blue

Rear-Admiral Horatio Nelson